Tranquil Mind

Tranquil Mind

AN INTRODUCTION TO BUDDHISM AND MEDITATION

Rob Nairn

KAIRON

This book is humbly dedicated to
His Holiness Ogyen Trinley Dorje
The 17th Karmapa

Foreword

Tranquil Mind is the first book on Buddhist philosophy and meditation written in South Africa. Its pioneering role in the growth of Buddhism in the region since its publication in 1993 is widely acknowledged. But its light has also spread far beyond the borders of Africa. In ten years it has become an international best seller, now available in eight languages. This is not only an abundant overflowing of Rob Nairn's original purpose but also an enduring testimony to his skill, clarity and popularity as a teacher.

I welcome this revised 10th anniversary edition, and pray that Rob and *Tranquil Mind* will continue to guide beings everywhere on their path of inner peace, clarity and compassion.

Dr Akong Tulku Rinpoche
Founder and President
Rokpa International
Charitable Trust

Kagyu Samye Ling Tibetan Centre
Eskdalemuir, Dumfriesshire
DG13 OQL
Scotland

First published in 1993 by Carrefour/Dragon Publications.
Second edition by Kairon Press in 1997.
Afrikaans translation by Karel Schoeman, *'n Stil Gemoed,* published in 1997.
Shambhala Publications, Boston, USA published the book as
What is meditation? Buddhism for everyone in 1999.

Published by Kairon Press CC
PO Box 100, Kalk Bay, 7990, South Africa
kairon@icon.co.za; www.icon.co.za/~kairon

NATURE PHOTOGRAPHS: © Donovan Kirkwood

DEDICATION PHOTOGRAPH: courtesy Rumtek monastery, Sikkim
COVER PHOTOGRAPH OF VAJRA ON AKONG RINPOCHE SEAT: Lindi Te Water
COVER DESIGN: Linda Vicquery & Anka of eye4design
EDITORIAL CONSULTANT: Miles Mattson
AUTHOR PHOTOGRAPH: Desmond Bowes Taylor
DESIGN AND LAYOUT: Damian Gibbs, Orchard Publishing
PRINTED AND BOUND: Formsxpress, Cape Town, South Africa

2004 hard cover ISBN 0-9584348-5-9

Preface 2004

Would you believe this little book has now been going for ten years? My publisher and I were so surprised we decided to have a celebratory Tenth Anniversary edition.

Here are a few interesting pieces of information:

- I wrote *Tranquil Mind* simply to help students gain a perspective on Buddhism and meditation. I never thought it would become a world-selling book. I am delighted and hope it continues to help many people.
- It has gone into many languages, eight to be precise. I think the biggest joy was when Karel Schoeman translated it into Afrikaans, and brought his wonderful classical mind to Buddhism.
- I am working on a Shona translation – my first major effort to translate Buddhism into an African language. Shona is the main language of Zimbabwe and I grew up with Shona people. A group of us are now working on the book. Wish us well in our efforts to bring the Dharma to Africa!

Preface 1993

This book has two purposes:

1. To introduce the reader to the essential principles of Buddhism.
2. To describe how to meditate in a way that anyone can understand and follow; basic meditation exercises for beginners are included.

In short, it is the answer to those who ask What is Buddhism all about? and What is Buddhist meditation?

In essence . . .

Buddhism is essentially a collection of skilful methods of working with the mind. If we understood and applied these to our lives, we would unfold our inherent ability to experience inner peace, compassion and wisdom by developing the basic potential of our minds.

This potential is within each of us and anyone can realise it by making the effort. Buddhists therefore have no sense of being different or unique.

The study and practice of Buddhism are not matters of custom. We do not have to sit in a particular way or wear special clothes, or appear in a certain way. Such superficial matters are of no importance.

The teachings are concerned with the diminishing and eventual elimination of our negative patterns, not changing our superficial appearance.

This book helps to guide us along that path.

Contents

Part One

An introduction to Buddhism

I

What is Buddhism?

To abstain from all evil
To cultivate every virtue
And to tame one's mind
This is the teaching of the Buddhas.

What is Buddhism?

Buddhism is a religion and a philosophy; but most of all, it is a way of life.

The historical Buddha – Sakyamuni, the sage of the Sakyas – lived and taught in North Central India approximately 2 500 years ago. Born as Prince Siddhartha Gautama, he abandoned all worldly possessions to practise radical asceticism. After realising that neither hedonism nor ascetism could give him the answers he sought, he decided to follow the Middle Way. He is seen as a great being who achieved his highest destiny: enlightenment.

The Buddha is not the name of a person; it is a title derived from the root *budh* – to wake. Thus *Buddha* literally means awakened, developed and enlightened, and the *Buddha* means the enlightened one.

The Buddha taught that every one of us has the same destiny, and can achieve it if we make the effort. The purpose of the Buddha's teaching is to guide us on the road to our enlightenment; hence it is to be applied to our daily living, not kept as an interesting theory. 'If you see a signpost on a road, follow it and you will reach your goal; if you sit down beneath it and gaze at it, you will get nowhere.'

The Buddha was not the first being ever to become enlightened, nor was he seen as unique or exceptional. He was a teacher and a friend who is still greatly respected because he brought to perfection the human qualities of purity, wisdom and compassion: but he is not a saviour, nor is he worshipped as a god. Statues and depictions of the Buddha are symbols reminding us that our true nature is the same as that of the Buddha – enlightened.

Tolerance

A cardinal feature of Buddhism is the emphasis on respect for the religions of others and tolerance of all people, regardless of race, creed or culture. It is above all, a religion of peace.

In the third century BCE, the Buddhist emperor Asoka carved in rock:

One should not honour only one's own religion and condemn the religions of others, but one should honour others' religions . . .
So doing, one helps one's own religion to grow and renders service to the religions of others too. In acting otherwise one digs the grave of one's own religion and also does harm to other religions . . .

Compassion and wisdom

The essence of the Buddha's teaching is compassion. Compassion is the discerning ability to help in an appropriate manner; it is not a sentimental emotion. It is vital active knowledge of what is appropriate in a given situation.

Compassion begins with being open first to ourselves, to our inner experience and thus accepting ourselves. Then we apply that openness to the world around us, to individuals, to events, to situations. Compassion is all-embracing caring that arises within the mind of an enlightened being, a caring which sees all forms of life and of beings as equal. It can only arise in a mind that is completely open, a mind that is not narrowed by preferences, judgements, intolerance, or by blocking off. We can all reach the stage of enlightened compassion; the first step is to start accepting ourselves and others without judgement.

The Buddha did not set out to found a religion or convert people to any belief system or dogma. His mission was to show people the way to liberation from sorrow and suffering. To this end he taught a system of ethical and altruistic living which he recommended to all people. The emphasis within the system is on refraining from any harmful or destructive behaviour, and engaging in every possible form of kind, loving and compassionate conduct.

The way to liberation includes teaching on meditation, which is a scientific system of relaxed reflection and mind culture that leads the practitioners to a direct experience of their true nature. A deepening of this experience calls forth the wisdom which is within all of us. Through meditation and reflection, compassion and wisdom blossom within the mind, leading to full enlightenment – liberation from any further possibility of suffering.

Impartiality

Buddhists are not taught to convert people to their way of thinking; they attempt to practise the Buddha's teachings and make them available to others who might benefit from them. Many people explore and apply these teachings to their lives while remaining committed to other religions or no religion.

Buddhism is not a cult: it is based upon one of the most highly developed and sophisticated philosophical systems known to humanity and is taught and respected in leading universities throughout the world. Throughout its history it has been supported and honoured by some of the world's greatest civilisations and cultures, and has brought peace, happiness and freedom to millions of people since the time of the Buddha. There is no record in history of a Buddhist religious war.

Refuge

Taking refuge is a commitment to one's own deepest spiritual welfare, to one's own wisdom nature. It does not mean taking shelter in something external.

Refuge is taken in the Buddha (the enlightened essence of compassion and wisdom within all of us), the *dharma* (the teaching that will help unfold the enlightened essence within) and the *sangha* (those realised people and other beings who can guide us on our inner path).

In its simplest form it is an affirmation of confidence and trust before meditation sessions. Longer and more formal refuge ceremonies conducted by a fully realised teacher, such as a lama[1], can very empowering, and are the seed of a blessing that will flower when the time and conditions are right.

---

[1] A lama is a spiritual teacher or mentor who cares for beings at the deepest possible level. *La* is an honorific indicating the highest respect, and *ma* means mother.

In essence taking refuge is a commitment of oneself to oneself to the spiritual path and a turning away from worldly refuges such as material possessions, career success and a solace in relationships. All the latter continue to have a place in our lives but are not given primary importance.

Schools of Buddhism

As with all major religions, Buddhism has a number of schools and lineages. These developed over many centuries, first in response to the needs of the laity in the southern countries. As Buddhism moved northwards the teachings took on cultural and psychological colouring appropriate to the country, while remaining faithful to the core doctrines: new ground, new growth, same seed.

There is no centralised world Buddhist authority, and different groups throughout the world are autonomous. Some groups are large with branches throughout the world; others are small and localised.

There are three main groups: Theravada, Mahayana and Vajrayana.

THERAVADA (THE TEACHING OF THE ELDERS)

Theravadin schools constitute the Southern Transmission, and are found in Burma, Indonesia, Cambodia, Laos, Sri Lanka and Thailand. They trace their origin to the period immediately following the passing of the Buddha when eighteen schools of early Buddhism developed. Of these, Theravada is the only modern survivor.

Theravadin Buddhism has two main areas of focus:

- The observance of strict ethical rules and the avoidance of all harm to others. As a result, it markedly emphasises the monastic life, and great respect is accorded monks and nuns.
- Understanding, through meditation and reflection, of the inherent emptiness of the personality. This is not an easy area of Buddhism to understand. The danger of failing to comprehend its subtleties has been likened to that of wrongly grasping a snake.

MAHAYANA (THE GREATER VEHICLE)

This school developed in the first century CE. The term Greater Vehicle distinguishes it from the contemporary Theravadin schools which were monastic and focused chiefly on self-liberation and thus came to be called Hinayana (Lesser Vehicle).

The Mahayana schools incorporate the teachings of Theravada, but in addition regard the *bodhisattva* ideal as of primary importance. A bodhisattva is one who does all for the benefit of others. He or she vows not to enter the state of final liberation (*nirvana*) but instead returns to the world to help others. Compassion and wisdom are emphasised. The place of lay practitioners is given importance.

On the subject of emptiness, Mahayana includes the Theravadin view of emptiness of personality, but goes further and teaches emptiness of object, or 'non-self of phenomena'. To be empty of a separate enduring identity means to be one with everything in the cosmos. Emptiness does not mean non-existence. It means co-existence with all that is. It is impermanence, it is change, it is life.

Mahayana schools are found in Taiwan, Japan, Mainland China, Tibet, India, Nepal, Indonesia and Korea. Within Mahayana are many well-known sub-schools such as Zen.

Vajrayana (the Diamond Vehicle) or Tantra

Tantric schools developed in North India between the third and seventh centuries CE. They incorporated the other two schools but added a further feature: rapid attainment of enlightenment through specialised forms of meditation which used visualisation and *mantra* (the chanting of sacred words). They developed and flourished chiefly in Tibet.

In Vajrayana a major shift of perspective is involved. The practitioner trains to recognise the fundamental purity of all phenomena, even though they appear otherwise. We are now in the realms of the most paradoxical Buddhist teachings on the nature of reality.

Tibetan Buddhism

There are four main lineages or schools in Tibetan Buddhism: Nyingma, Sakya, Karma Kagyu and Gelugpa. The present Dalai Lama, the best-known Buddhist in the modern world, is the spiritual head of the Gelukpas. He is also the political head of the Tibetan government-in-exile. He was granted political asylum in India after the Chinese takeover of Tibet in 1959 and established a Tibetan village in Dharamsala, North India.

The Karmapa is head of the Karma Kagyu lineage. The 17th Karmapa, Ogyen Trinley Dorje, escaped from his traditional seat, Tsurphu monastery, in Tibet in 2 000 at the age of 15. Currently he has 'refugee' status in India, where he is living as guest of the Dalai Lama at the Gyuto Tantric University. The main seat of the Karmapa in India is Rumtek monastery, Sikkim and in the West it is Karma Triyana Dharmachakra (KTD) in Woodstock, New York.

The Awakening of the West

During his lifetime the Buddha gave a great variety of teachings to suit every human condition and level of understanding. In classical Buddhism this body of teachings came to be divided into three major 'turnings of the wheel of dharma', each marking an advance in the level of instruction and comprehension. But the story does not end with the death of the Buddha 2 500 years ago.

Historically there are many accounts of the bodhisattva activities of the Buddha in previous lives. The early Mahayana school saw no reason to think that this cycle of enlightened activity ended with the Buddha's physical passing, and so he came to take on a transcendent but very real aspect of continuous manifestation in an often turbulent and chaotic world. Viewed in this light, the later *sutras*[2] and the spread and development of Mahayana, Zen and Vajrayana schools in Asia may be regarded as a further major turning of the wheel. In our own time, the consequences of the Chinese invasion and occupation of Tibet in 1959 seem no less significant. It was predicted long ago in Tibet that 'when the iron bird flies, the buddhadharma will move West'.

---

[2] Sutras: Texts containing the dialogues and discourses of the Buddha, although written down only many years after his passing. A sutra literally is a thread on which jewels are strung.

A mere 100 years ago most Europeans and Americans were totally ignorant of Buddhism and only a few scholars had any coherent grasp of its teachings. Today its adherents are counted in the millions in Western and Eastern Europe and North America, and its growth in Australia, New Zealand and parts of Africa has been marked during the past thirty years. Many Buddhist meditation centres, libraries, retreat centres, universities and communities have now been established in these countries.

This has prepared the ground for a new and potentially fruitful engagement between science and religion, whose orthodox positions have long been regarded as fundamentally irreconcilable. In the past decade there has been an unprecedented level of interaction between Western science and the world's wisdom traditions, in which Buddhist lamas, philosophers, meditators and writers have been prominent[3]. The integration of the sciences and spiritual knowledge has profound implications for the future of humanity. From the Buddhist point of view it may well be that this is the next great turning of the wheel of dharma.

[3] A conspicuous example of this sort of contact is the two-day conference at the Massachusetts Institute of Technology in September 2003, presided over by the Dalai Lama. It quickly sold out to an international audience of about 1,200 luminaries, mainly scientists, and racked up a waiting list of 1,600. It has been described as 'a watershed'.

2

The Buddha's Teaching

Although I have shown the means of liberation,
you must know that it depends on you alone.
– The Buddha

The Four Noble Truths

The heart of the Buddha's teaching lies in the Four Noble Truths which he expounded in his first teaching at Sarnath, also referred to as the First Turning of the Wheel of Dharma. They are:

1. Unsatisfactoriness of worldly conditions – *dukkha* (sometimes expressed as 'suffering')
2. The arising or origin of unsatisfactoriness – *samudaya*
3. The cessation of unsatisfactoriness – *nirodha*
4. The way leading to cessation – *magga*

The First Noble Truth: Unsatisfactoriness (Suffering)

The Buddha taught that life in this world (*samsara*) is essentially unsatisfactory because it does not offer what we most want – permanent and unchanging happiness, harmony and comfort– that which we would conventionally describe as nirvana. Although worldly life can sometimes produce these states, we cannot pass beyond the reach of suffering while we are in the world; this is because our consciousness is blinded by desire and worldly perspectives which fail to take account of the fact that everything within the world is impermanent and will come to an end sooner or later. The happiness that is built on the sands of impermanence will therefore collapse when the sands shift – as they surely will.

Although this situation is obvious to anyone who thinks about it, very few people realise it because we are all so caught up in pursuing our short-term worldly goals that we seldom stop to think about the larger perspectives of our lives:

> *What is really going on?*
> *What are we doing with our lives?*
> *Are we achieving anything of value in the long term?*

If we reflect on these greater issues we soon realise that our lives are generally very limited; we tend to repeat the same patterns and cycles like rats running around in a maze. We don't learn from life and therefore make the same mistakes over and over again – searching for happiness in the same unlikely places and suffering disappointment and sadness over and over again. This is the cycle, which is illustrated in a rather funny story.

There was once a great Sufi master who used to teach his students in many different and sometimes bizarre ways. One evening they arrived at his house to find him crawling around on the ground. There was a lamp by the front door and he was moving around within the lamplight.

> 'Master, what are you doing?'
> *'Searching for the front door key.'*
> They all joined him, crawling around, hunting for the key. After quite a long period of fruitless search, one student asked –
> 'Master, where were you when you lost the key?'
> *'Over there.'* He pointed to a distant spot which was in darkness.
> 'Then why on earth are you hunting for it here?'
> *'Oh, because it's so much easier to hunt here in the light.'*

This is what we all tend to do. Due to ignorance and confusion we strive to find happiness in places where it cannot be found. We keep on doing this because superficial appearances delude us into thinking that it can be found where we seek it – within the world of desire and the senses. Happiness cannot truly be found there, so our efforts lead instead to suffering.

No-self

The concept of no-self or egolessness (*anatta*) distinguishes Buddhism from all other major religions.

Anatta, the bold assertion that there is no independently existing self or soul, radically challenges our deeply rooted sense of separate egocentric identity. It also has profound implications for the way we choose to live our lives.

Buddhism neither seeks nor needs the validation of modern science, but growing contact between the two has revealed striking parallels between their respective views on the ultimate nature of the material universe and, even more surprisingly in modern neuroscience, on the nature of consciousness, the illusion of 'self' and 'other', and the possibility of waking up from a dream-like state of confusion.

After 2 500 years, the essentially Buddhist doctrine of anatta is engaging the serious attention of scientists whose attitude of skeptical inquiry seems to be in keeping with the Buddha's advice not to accept any teaching – even his own – without personal verification through direct experience.

The next step is for science to accept that although it is making huge strides in investigating consciousness, it cannot provide all the tools necessary for the direct understanding of spiritual truths.

For direct experience and understanding we have to learn to meditate.

But let's get back to the concept of no-self.

The important question is – who or what is it that suffers? This raises one of the most important aspects of the Buddha's teaching. He discovered through deep meditation that what we call me, self, i, is actually not a static, self-existent entity at all, even though we think of it in that way. One could understand this point by thinking of a candle flame. When you light a candle, a flame burns; this flame is there and has an appearance. Walk away and return five minutes later. There is still a flame burning. Is it the flame you saw earlier? No. It is a successor, because a flame is constantly changing. So what you have is appearance without solid substance or 'i-ness'. This point becomes more obvious if you blow the flame out: there is then nothing. Conclusion? A flame has no enduring or intrinsic 'selfness'. We only talk of a flame as long as there is a flickering appearance dancing on the candle wick. If it had 'selfness' there would be something left when the flame is extinguished, but there isn't. So the important point we learn from this illustration is that there can be appearance without substance, or a manifestation of energy which is not a 'self-in-itself'.

There is a second equally important point: the appearance (flame) can only come into being if some other condition exists first – in this case the candle and obviously the match that ignites it. The flame's existence is thus dependent on something else. Once again this emphasises that there is no self-existing 'flame-self': only an appearance that manifests when certain conditions are present – its appearance is dependent upon those conditions.

Our appearance in the world is not unlike this. What we call self is a combination of ever-changing physical and mental forces or energies which are divided up into five groups or aggregates. The Buddha said 'In short these five aggregates of attachment are dukkha.'. So the five aggregates and dukkha are not two different things; the five aggregates themselves are dukkha. What are these five?

Some of the following material is taken from *What the Buddha taught.*[4]

[4] Walpola Rahula, Grove Press, New York, 1962.

The Five Aggregates (skandhas)

1. Matter or Form. This includes the four elements – earth, water, fire, wind; also the six sense organs and their corresponding objects in the world:

   eye – visible form
   ear – sound
   nose – smell
   mouth – taste
   skin – sensation
   mind – thoughts, perceptions, feelings

   Note that the Buddha classified mind as a sense organ along with the five physical ones. So we have six senses.
2. Sensations. All our sensations – pleasant, neutral or unpleasant – experienced through the contact of physical and mental organs with the external world.
3. Perceptions. They arise in relation to the six senses. It is perceptions that give rise to recognition.
4. Mental Formations. Often called volitional activity (that is intentional acts; acts performed out of choice). This element in the personality directs the mind in the sphere of positive, negative or neutral activities, and produces karmic effects.
5. Consciousness. This is a reaction or response connected to one of the six senses, and constitutes a form of awareness. For example, when the eye comes into contact with a colour, visual consciousness arises. This is simply awareness of

colour; it does not recognise the colour – it is perception that causes recognition.

What does all this mean to us? It means the aggregates are like building materials which come together when we appear in the world. Just as building materials determine the nature of a building – for example stones and tiles produce a stone building with a tiled roof – so it is that the aggregates determine the nature of what we call 'me'. Because these five have come together due to karmic forces, an appearance has arisen. The aggregates are the condition (like the candle) which has made the appearance (the flame) possible. Due to the nature of this appearance a sense of self or me has arisen. This is you and i. This idea of 'i' gives rise to egocentricity – the sense of me here and everything else other out there. Because there is egocentricity, there is craving and grasping – 'i want'. And then all the trouble begins.

Enlightenment

But this explanation still does not clarify everything, because we might conclude that when the aggregates finally dissolve, we get snuffed out like the candle – nothing left! This is nihilism which the Buddha said was a grave misunderstanding of the way things are.

The situation is not like that. In reality, each one of us exists, always has existed, and always will exist as an enlightened being. Enlightenment is a state beyond human understanding and words can give only a hint of what it means – it is the state free from negative or conflicting emotions, free from any sense of duality, free from any form of negativity or ignorance. In that state, every positive or perfect condition is fully and naturally present – perfect love, compassion, joy, happiness and equanimity. This is the true nature of all beings; this is 'reality'.

This is what stands behind the illusion of 'me' that arises due to the manifestation of the aggregates. This is the state we experience and realise when we finally relinquish our egocentric grasping and pass forever beyond the illusion of a separate self. It is not until this happens that we will finally be free of suffering – dukkha.

The Second Noble Truth: Origin or Arising

The arising or origin of dukkha is thirst or craving. It is this energy of desire that sets in motion a 'cycle of becoming' in which beings become trapped. What seems to happen is that craving becomes involved with the sense of self – the one who craves. This sense of self, or separation, is an inaccurate understanding of life and gives rise to egocentric grasping. This inaccurate understanding is ignorance. So we live in a state of fundamental ignorance as to the true nature of what we are and what the world is. Because of this we act out of ignorance and confusion: we live to serve egocentric interests and seek constantly to gratify egocentric craving. Driven by the neurotic energy caused by this, we perform harmful acts of body, speech and mind, and thus generate negative karma which ripens into suffering for ourselves and others.

This grasping is driving us all the time, but we are so accustomed to it that we do not recognise it for what it is, and take it for granted. While it remains unrecognised, it retains its power over us and gets ever stronger, keeping us in constant bondage to our senses and perpetuating pain and suffering in our lives. This situation can only be brought to an end when, through the development of wisdom and compassion, we begin to recognise the patterns of egocentric craving and grasping, see them as harmful and systematically let go of them. This is why we need to meditate.

The Third Noble Truth: CESSATION

Stated simply, the cessation of dukkha can be brought about. How? By giving up egocentric grasping. This entails getting directly in touch with the ignorance and desire that cause grasping, seeing it for what it is, and letting it go. Then nirvana – extinction of thirst – is experienced. Because nirvana is an absolute, it is impossible to describe and is thus usually alluded to in terms of what is no longer there.

Sariputra, the chief student of the Buddha, defined nirvana as 'the extinction of desire, the extinction of hatred, the extinction of illusion'. Those three – desire, hatred and illusion – are referred to as the three mind poisons which dominate our minds and drive us to negative and destructive behaviour. When we free ourselves from their grip, we free ourselves from suffering. What then remains is the purest form of happiness.

The Fourth Noble Truth: The Way

The path is the Middle Way. It is the way of balance, good sense and no extremes. There are two extremes into which both worldly people and practitioners fall. First – hedonism: the search for happiness through the pleasures of the senses. This does not work because it is degrading, dissipates vital human energy, and ultimately leads to greater suffering and bondage. The second is the search for happiness through self-mortification and extreme asceticism – not so common in the West, but apparently popular in India in the time of the Buddha. This route is not only painful, but also pointless, unproductive and obviously a path of suffering. Through his own efforts and personal experience, the Buddha discovered the Middle Way 'which gives vision and knowledge; which leads to calm, insight, enlightenment, nirvana'.

In other words – permanent happiness and freedom from all forms of suffering.

Like the Buddha, most of us first encounter the Middle Way as a need to exercise sensible moderation at the level of our personal desires, inclinations and habits; for example, not eating too much or too little, or finding a healthy balance between work and play.

But the Buddhist concept of the Middle Way extends like a golden thread through all levels of life. It embraces all aspects of private and public morality, ethics and conduct. It includes the wise ordering of government under law, proper care of the environment, the economical and benevolent use of natural resources, fairness in work and employment, and generosity in the sharing of prosperity. It is the antithesis of the egocentric greed and grasping that poisons human existence.

Buddhism does not teach that one has to shun wealth and the enjoyment of this life in order to obtain liberation. Indeed, accounts of the lives and legends of great yogis contain examples of how gurus have transformed the grasping love of wealth and luxury in kings and princes into instruments leading to their enlightenment and consequent generosity, greatly benefitting their subjects.

At profoundly deeper levels, the Middle Way is the balance of wisdom and compassion, the way of the bodhisattva.

The Middle Way has eight components, so is known as:

The Noble Eightfold Path

1. Right Understanding
2. Right Thought
3. Right Speech
4. Right Action
5. Right Livelihood
6. Right Effort
7. Right Mindfulness
8. Right Meditation

The eight are listed in an order which has a logic of its own, but this does not mean that one 'Right' has to be fully mastered before one can pass on to the next. It is necessary to attend simultaneously to all areas, but a thorough grounding in the first two will certainly help motivate a person to practise the others.

The Eightfold Path sets out a comprehensive framework for bringing all areas of one's activity into line with principles which create inner and outer harmony. They are guides for avoiding destructive activity which leads to suffering for oneself and others, and engaging in activities of body, speech and mind that will lead to happiness and liberation. The main principle is actually very simple – do not do, think or say anything harmful and engage all your energy in beneficial acts, and the result is inevitable: happiness for yourself and others, and, ultimately, enlightenment.

The problem is that on the one hand many beings do not believe in cause and effect, so they do not connect their sufferings and misfortunes with previous harmful acts, or their present happiness and good fortune with previous beneficial acts. Because of this they are not motivated to do good and avoid harm. On the other hand, even where this motivation is present, there is often such confusion in the mind that beings are unable to distinguish fully between harmful and unharmful activity. As a result, the Eightfold Path is not so easy to follow.

In order to address this difficulty, it is valuable to begin by reflecting on the nature of life so as to dispel confused and unrealistic beliefs and attitudes, while at the same time acquiring a more accurate understanding of the way things really are. There are many systems of reflection within Buddhist philosophy, some of which are quite elaborate, but the main points are contained within four basic reflections.

The Four Reflections that Turn the Mind

These are known as the four reflections that turn the mind from the path of suffering. At first these reflections may seem a bit strange and simplistic, but if one spends a bit of time on them, their inherent truth penetrates the confused and deluded mind, giving rise to a more realistic and workable approach to life. Out of this a deep motivation to do something about one's situation grows.

These reflections are outlined here. They are fully expounded in such works as *The Torch of Certainty* by Jamgon Kongtrul the Great.[5]

1. PRECIOUS HUMAN BIRTH

Reflect that your situation in the world is such that you actually have an opportunity to break forever the chain of causality which keeps you in the cycle of suffering or unsatisfactoriness. You have time to devote to your spiritual training, resources to support yourself while doing so, and access to teachings and teachers which will enable you to do what is necessary to liberate yourself. In addition, you have some inclination to follow a spiritual path – it is unlikely you would be reading these words if this were not so. This combination of factors is rare. If you doubt this, compare yourself with the vast majority of people in

[5] Judith Hansom & Shambhala Publications, Boston, USA, 1977.

the world: most are either engaged in a struggle for survival, or are committed to pursuing the things of this world. Either way, they are unable or disinclined to follow a spiritual discipline and thus do not have the chance to benefit themselves in a real way. Regarded from this perspective, what you have is exceptional and rare – even more so when you think of the number of mammals, insects and reptiles in the world who would also like to free themselves from suffering but have no way to do so. This is why your present birth is called 'precious'. You have an opportunity which is very rare – like a rare diamond: that's precious! The conclusion is – use it while you have it.

2. Impermanence

Everything in the universe we know is impermanent and will pass away sooner or later. This applies particularly to this fortunate birth which we have. We do not know when the hour will arrive for our death, and it may be sooner than we expect. Therefore resolve now to use the opportunity you have to liberate yourself, to the full. If you do this, when you die you will not have any regrets about wasted opportunities, and you will know that your life has been worthwhile.

3. Karma – cause and effect

Everything we experience is governed by the law of cause and effect. The Buddha taught that we have been taking rebirth in different realms for millions of aeons. During this time we will have performed many negative as well as positive actions. We do not know when the consequences of these negative actions are going to manifest, and how they will manifest. What we are told is that there are many states into which we can be reborn as a result of past karma; some are pleasant, others are very uncomfortable and best avoided.

The best way to ensure our future happiness is to embark seriously on the path of spiritual training now while we have the opportunity. When we lose this body, it might be a very long time before we obtain another one, so we have no time to lose.

4. The unsatisfactoriness of samsara

As was said at the beginning of this section, the world in which we live is ultimately not going to give us the peace and happiness we long for. On the contrary, it seems to hold hidden dangers beyond imagining. The road to lasting happiness is to explore and give expression to the true, enlightened nature that lies within every one of us. There is no point in delaying the spiritual endeavour which this calls for.

Students are generally advised to begin their spiritual journey by reflecting on these four topics daily, until a true realisation of the importance of a spiritual discipline begins to take hold in the mind. Until this happens, the mind will remain obsessed with the outer world, and there will be a continuing conviction that permanent happiness can be found 'out there'. It is only when we stand back and view the situation intelligently and reflectively that we deeply realise that we have to turn within, develop our inner strength, unfold our true nature. This is the spiritual path. Having worked with the mind in this way, we develop an accurate understanding of the external world and our own nature. This understanding makes it easier to give up desire, craving, grasping for outer things. Against this background we become motivated to tread the Noble Eightfold Path in a consistent and intelligent way.

When we begin practising, we develop the eight stages more or less simultaneously, according to our individual capacity. We soon discover that they are all interconnected, and each helps the development of the others. The practice of these eight perfects the three essentials of Buddhist training and discipline:

1. Ethical conduct
2. Mental discipline
3. Wisdom.

Ethical conduct is built on the vast conception of universal love and compassion for all living beings, on which the Buddha's teaching is based. The Buddha gave his teachings for the good of the many, for the happiness of the many, out of compassion for the world. According to Buddhism, for a person to be perfect there are two qualities that should be developed equally: compassion on one side and wisdom on the other.

A great deal has been written about the Path but the basic purpose of this teaching is always to be kept in mind – it expounds a way of life to be followed, practised and developed by each individual. It is self-discipline in body, word and mind; self-development and self-purification.

If the teachings are applied, enlightenment will follow.

This ends the discussion of the Four Noble Truths and the Noble Eightfold Path. They constitute the core of the Buddha's teaching. Although many philosophical issues are contained within them, their true purpose was and is practical: they were offered as a framework within which we can do something which will benefit ourselves and others, which will lead us all to lasting happiness and freedom from suffering.

Interdependent origination

When this is, that is
This arising, that arises
When this is not, that is not
This ceasing, that ceases.

When we were children, many of us played with dominoes. You can stand them on end and arrange them in a pattern, each one within falling distance of the one behind it. Then push the first one over – it flattens the second which flattens the third and so on. Eventually they are all down. Why? Because of their relationship to each other, and then because the first one was knocked over. This is the principle of dependent origination – when certain causes are set in motion, others inevitably follow because they are linked as in a chain. There are twelve links in this chain:

1. Ignorance
2. Intentional actions
3. Consciousness
4. Body and mind
5. Six sense organs and their objects
6. Contact
7. Sensation
8. Desire

9. Grasping (attachment – drawing to 'self')
10. Becoming – existence
11. Rebirth
12. Sickness, old age and death.

These twelve account for our predicament in this world. Due to ignorance (which is the first domino) a whole lot of other things come into being. This is the cycle:

1. Through ignorance, intentional egocentric actions are performed (in service of the mistaken idea of a self).
2. Intentional actions tend to be repeated many times and thus form habits in the mind. These habits pass into consciousness as conditioning.
3. This conditioned consciousness exists in this form only due to the habits brought about by repeated actions (of body, speech or mind). This is termed *karmic creation*. Conditioned consciousness links with an embryo in the womb and leads to the fourth stage:
4. Body and mind. These would not exist if karmically conditioned consciousness had not first come into being. When body and mind exist, they are accompanied by:
5. The six sense organs and their objects (referred to a little earlier) – for example the eye and visual objects. When these two sets come into existence, then there is automatically:

6. Contact – for example the sense of taste and that which is tasted. This causes:
7. Sensation. If it is tasty food, the sensation will be pleasant and one will want to repeat it. Thus there will be the arising of:
8. Desire, leading to:
9. Grasping. If i desire something, i want to get it, so i grasp at it. The consequence of this is:
10. Coming into existence. In the external world this means drawing things to me so that possessions etcetera come into existence. There is now a distinct sense of 'beingness' or 'me-ness' which seems to develop because where there is grasping, the idea arises of one who grasps. This consciousness leads to:
11. Rebirth. Because everything is impermanent, everything born is subject to:
12. Sickness, old age and death.

This is the full cycle. No sooner has this course been run than it starts up again due to the continuing presence of ignorance. This cycle can go on forever, and will do so if we do not do something about it.

We are experiencing this cycle incessantly in our lives without realising it. Through meditation and mind culture (which includes reflecting) we create space in the mind which enables us to see directly what we had previously not seen. This is called insight. Insight reveals our compulsive patterns of grasping at every level of thought, feeling and activity. This grasping manifests incessantly in the service of a supposed self and leads inevitably to suffering. It only happens because in our ignorance we believe there is a self. The first major step towards enlightenment is taken when we actually experience the fact that there is no actual 'me' – only a stream of consciousness which is manifesting various characteristics. When this experience stabilises, we break the wheel of twelve links because the delusion is dispelled.

Intellectualism

This emphasises one of the most important aspects of Buddhism – one that many people never fully grasp: intellectual understanding of the teachings helps to the extent that it dispels misconceptions about life, and it therefore has value. But in terms of the journey, it is only the signpost. The real spiritual journey begins only when we start meditating and reflecting; these activities bring us into direct contact with what is happening at an inner level, and lead to true experience, understanding and awakening of wisdom. There is no substitute for this, and nobody can progress spiritually without embarking on this experiential journey. The spiritual path is a 'hands on' business, not a comfortable intellectualisation of life. Intellectualisation is usually employed as a defence by people who cannot accept or face themselves at a level of feeling – and meditation takes us straight into our feelings – so they end up sitting forlornly beneath the signpost.

This ends the subject of interdependent origination, which the Buddha taught to show that as long as there is ignorance and egocentric grasping, we will be tied to the wheel of birth and death. The way to freedom is to break the chain.

KARMA AND REINCARNATION

Within us is the potential to be whatever we choose.
– Akong Rinpoche

These two concepts are now familiar to most people who have an interest in meditation – they contain the laws of how things are, and are not the unique province of Buddhism. Many Eastern religions include an understanding of them, and many books are available on the subject, so it will not be expounded here. However, two points should be made to remove common misconceptions:

Karma does not mean punishment. It is the Law of Cause and Effect. If you want to grow a cabbage, you plant a cabbage seed (cause) and a cabbage grows (effect). If you plant an acorn hoping for a cabbage, you will get an oak tree instead. This may cause you disappointment, but it is not a punishment. It is a simple consequence of what you did. This is what life is all about. We all want to be happy, but do many things which are unskillful and produce negative effects in our minds and in our environment. These are the basis of our suffering and unhappiness.

Nobody has done anything to us – we have done it to ourselves. We are heir to our karma. We are also masters of our destiny, because with a bit of care we can eliminate harmful acts which produce painful results, and practise positive or kind acts which produce happiness. This is why the Buddha emphasised the importance of ethical and altruistic behaviour – it leads to happiness. The most important thing in all the world is to be kind.

Reincarnation largely traces the changes within the mind due to karmic forces. These changes produce states which we experience as 'solid'. A depressed person is in a different world from a happy person. A paranoid person is in a hell realm, while a person who intentionally ignores the implications of his or her actions, is in an animal realm – different realms, different manifestations. When we die it is these states of mind that go on and manifest naturally in forms which most appropriately express what is there. It is therefore a fallacy to assume that future births will necessarily be an improvement on the present – they depend on what we are doing now, how we are using our energy now. So we have to work now to improve the mind.

Compassion: the Bodhisattva ideal

The Buddha is often referred to as the Compassionate One because his life was a total manifestation of compassion, and the underlying emphasis of his teaching was on this topic. For this reason the Mahayana and Vajrayana schools emphasise it as the quality which needs to be developed above all, and without which no real spiritual progress is possible. Every aspect of meditation and training within these schools begins and ends by focusing on compassion as the motivation for practice. This attitude is fully developed in the bodhisattva ideal – the undertaking to tread the path to enlightenment with all the effort and hardship that entails, in order to help to liberate others.

Many serious practitioners take the bodhisattva vow, which is a vow to work tirelessly throughout this and all future lives, to reach enlightenment for the benefit of others: once having reached the level of enlightenment, not to pass away from samsara (the manifest universe in which we are trapped within the wheel of cyclic existence), but to remain among suffering beings and help them until they have all been liberated. This is a mighty undertaking, but it reflects the total commitment which the Buddha and his followers have to the welfare of all sentient beings – not just humans, but all sentient beings. It also expresses the greater Buddhist perspective, that we are not separate individuals; we are part of a great one-ness that ultimately transcends all duality. The bodhisattva works to manifest this truth.

Summary of the Buddha's teaching

The essential principles of Buddhism are contained in the topics discussed above: the Four Noble Truths, the Noble Eightfold Path, no-self, interdependent origination, the five aggregates, karma and reincarnation, compassion and the bodhisattva ideal. These of course do not account for all that the Buddha taught in his forty-five years of teaching. But if they are understood and applied, then the Buddhist path to liberation will reveal itself.

To conclude this chapter it may be helpful to look at all this from another perspective – that of distinguished biologists and other healthily skeptical academics who, like the Sufi master in the story told earlier, are beginning to see that lost keys are not always to be found in the convenient light of empirical science.

How the 'self' spins its own endless story

Increasingly, modern science is asking: is this oh-so-solid ego-belief really any more than an ever-changing fiction that is endlessly replicating itself like a virus in the infinitely complex matrix of the human brain?

This hypothesis that self-replicating units of imitation (called *memes*) establish habitual pathways in the mind accords closely with classic Buddhist texts on interdependent origination. It also echoes the words of the present Dalai Lama, who talks about how we 'often find ourselves hit by a sudden thought or feeling, such as fear, which, if we leave it to itself, without paying much attention, can begin to work in its own cause and affect us.'[6]

If our egocentric existence is no more than a story the mind tells itself about itself, then the notion of acting mainly out of self-interest becomes pointless and even ridiculous. This 'turning in the deepest seat of consciousness' is the beginning of what Tibetans call *rangjung*, spontaneously arising compassion for all sentient beings, balanced by the insight of wisdom.

This too, of course, begins as just another idea, another potential mind virus or 'memeplex'. But the difference is that by consciously paying impartial attention to everything that is happening in the moment, no matter what it is, we can end our habitual runaway cycles of self-replicating thoughts and emotions. The mind then begins to access a place of calm abiding where things just seem to work themselves out without the false idea that someone inside is doing it.

Miracles happen when we get our self-cherishing out of the way.

So we are back to meditation, one of the most important aspects of Buddhism.

---

[6] *The Power of Compassion*, Thorsons, London, 1995.

Part Two

An introduction to Meditation

3

Meditation

Meditation is the art of abandoning our delusions.
– Khentin Tsultrim Rinpoche

The importance of attitude

Meditation is unlike normal business or worldly activity because it is not goal-oriented and does not involve linear or directed thinking. It begins as a process of allowing the busy day-to-day mind with all its agitation, aggression, anger, fear and anxiety, to slow down and come to rest of its own accord. Most people do not know what causes this slowing down and coming to rest, so they do not know how to go about it.

What counts most in meditation is attitude.

If you have an attitude of wanting to achieve something, or change something within the mind, this will prevent meditation and result instead in mental conflict and tension. For example, many people think that the purpose of meditation is to make the mind go blank, or to stop thought, or in some way control or manipulate inner mental or emotional processes. They thus sit down expecting to be able to do this rather like King Canute sitting enthroned on the seashore ordering the tides back. The result is the same – instead of leading to inner peace, this attitude will cause a build-up of tension and suppressed emotional energy which will eventually burst upon consciousness and cause confusion.

Acceptance

An attitude of self-acceptance is essential to meditation. This begins with the mind; learning to accept everything that is happening within the mind – all the thoughts, all the feelings, whatever – and coming to terms with it. Any attitude of wanting to change or manipulate the mind, or enforce a different mind state constitutes non-acceptance and will lead to trouble. This makes sense if you think about it. If you had to live with someone who did not accept you as you were, but was always trying to change you, manipulate you, or mould you into their idea of what you should be, you would not like it and would feel uncomfortable, rejected and eventually rebellious. In the end your relationship with that person would be a bad one, full of conflict and tension.

Working with the mind is the same, because the mind is what we think of as me or self. If there is no inner acceptance then there is no basis for inner harmony and peace.

Stated simply, when we talk of acceptance, we are talking of unconditional love – starting with ourselves. If we are unable to accept and love ourselves unconditionally, then we will not be able to accept and love others; if we reject ourselves and live in a state of inner emotional conflict, confusion and tension, this is what we will put into the world around us because we manifest what we are. If we learn to accept and love ourselves unconditionally, then this is what we will manifest in the world. We will become happy, peaceful and loving, and will naturally express those qualities.

People often misunderstand acceptance and think it implies approval or endorsement of negative mind states. For example, most children are told that it is bad to be angry or to hate people, and so on. They grow up with an attitude that these states are unacceptable or dangerous ('I will be condemned and rejected and therefore not loved if I have these feelings'). This creates a quandary within the mind because practically everyone has these negative states to some degree. Normally the solution to this quandary is to ignore them and pretend they are not there, even to the point of denying their very existence. We do this with all our negative 'unacceptable' thoughts and feelings, following some irrational belief that if we do this long and hard enough, they will go away.

That is not the way things happen. This attitude produces nothing but inner conflict, chronic tension, anxiety, fear, neurosis, physical illness and eventually insanity. These negative states will not go away until we do something about them.

It is true that they are harmful. They are destructive; they do cause suffering to ourselves and others; they are the cause of all the trouble in the world. Happiness, peace and love are not possible while they are present within the mind. But how are they to be dealt with if suppression, denial and manipulation only make the situation worse? The solution is acceptance – the opposite of what most people think. Let us use an analogy.

If you are sick you go to a doctor. His first job is to diagnose the nature of your illness. This means he has to accept that you are sick. This does not mean he approves of sickness or says it is a good thing. It is just that until he accepts the fact, he cannot do anything about it. If he told you that sickness is bad and wrong, and that you should go home and stop being silly, you would go instead to another doctor. The doctor's function is to accept you as you are, examine you to determine what is wrong, make a diagnosis and then prescribe a cure.

That's what is meant by acceptance. Accept yourself as you are, because meditation will uncover at increasingly deep levels what is going on in the mind, and you cannot come to terms with the situation until there has been acceptance.

This is what is meant by attitude. Where there is acceptance, a great strength and flexibility arise in the mind. The narrow, brittle mind that cannot deal with life will be transformed and a broadness and openness will develop. This is the beginning of love and compassion. Without these qualities, meditation is not possible. Most of us do not have them, so we develop them as we progress along the path of spiritual endeavour. This topic has been dealt with at the beginning of this section because it is the most important aspect of meditation and best be kept in mind all the time. It is the context within which everything else takes place.

Meditation: How to begin

The premise we begin with is that every human being has great potential which can be realised. Each one of us is capable of experiencing a permanent state of total joy, love, clarity and openness; a state usually referred to as being beyond description because our ideas and concepts of human experience are inadequate to encompass it. This state is the experience of our true nature: of liberation; liberation from suffering in all its forms and manifestations. It is towards this end that for thousands of years people have been meditating.

For reasons which will be examined later, we have gone astray or missed the point of living. Through fundamentally misunderstanding what life is all about, we have focused our attention on a limited aspect of our conscious experience, and this has warped and distorted our view and therefore our experience of reality. This warping has led us into paths of egocentric fixation which have resulted in a variety of negative states. These negative states have taken hold in our consciousness at both gross and subtle levels and therefore have manifested in our minds either permanently or occasionally. When they manifest we suffer, because they are always painful – painful to ourselves (such as depression and jealousy), and often to others (such as anger and hatred when acted out).

So we meditate in order to create the conditions which will bring about a change in this state of affairs. The meditation exposes the fraud: it reveals the state of egocentric fixation.

Through it we discover that we are actually clinging to ways of being at a psychological level which are unhealthy, confusing and destructive. This discovery automatically leads to letting go and liberation, because we are working with our energies at fundamental, not theoretical levels. When we enter into true meditative states we experience the capacity of the mind to work with great clarity and immediacy – conditions which lead to profound transformations of consciousness. Change comes at this level because there is no inner debate or confusion. There is a clear seeing, and at the inner level, seeing is the action. Rather like the state of mind, if you can imagine it, of walking into a dimly-lit room and picking up what appears to be a piece of rope lying on the floor. No sooner have you taken hold of it, than you realise it is actually a snake. This realisation gives rise to a state of mind (except in cases of extreme neurosis) which is extremely clear and immediate: without an instant of debate or confusion, the mind says 'drop it!' and you drop it without having to think. We are talking here of a state of mind which arises through direct realisation, not through theory or debate. This is the quality of the meditative mind. (In this context, mind includes not only the intellectual thinking and reasoning faculty, but also feeling and emotion.)

The implication is not that we are all sunk in an endless ocean of permanent misery, anger and hatred; rather our lives are an unsatisfactory mixture of states and experiences which hardly ever actually fulfil our expectations. When our desires are fulfilled, the sense of fulfilment and satisfaction does not last. Before long we want more of the same again. So most of us have a sense of not being fulfilled, of skating on the surface of life – not achieving anything. It is these and similar feelings that lead us to the path of meditation: a path which leads to our own depths, away from external superficiality to inner realisation and total fulfilment.

WHAT IS MEDITATION?

Meditation is the process of learning to work skillfully with the mind in a way which will lead by successive stages to tranquillity, insight, spontaneous purification and total liberation from all negative states. This final stage is accompanied by full and total realisation of one's wholesome or 'divine' potential. Along the way one sees through the egocentric trap and springs it. As the process of inner discovery progresses, so the state of one's inner life improves. Inner harmony, clarity and stability come about; the confused, scattered mind is left behind, and one's life becomes happier, more joyous, open, giving and loving. The culmination is enlightenment – a word a little like *infinity* or *eternity*: we have a rough idea what is meant, but cannot actually grasp the full meaning. But it is certainly a state of joy which passes all understanding.

There are, of course, many different systems and methods of meditation, each having its own very particular purpose and result – one does not just 'meditate' any more than one would just walk into a motor sales room and order 'a vehicle'. If one buys a vehicle, one is quite specific about it: one does not buy a Mini to pull a plough, any more than one thinks of entering the Grand Prix on a tractor. So with meditation. If one wants to have psychedelic trips, space out, or go astral travelling, one then selects and applies the appropriate method or system.

However, this book is not about any of those processes. What will be dealt with here is one of the oldest and best tried systems of meditation known to humanity – commonly called *insight meditation.* This term derives from the basic method of meditation taught by the Buddha, called *Vipassana.* This word is usually translated as 'insight' or 'seeing things as they are'. More correctly it is called *Satipatthana meditation,* because it is derived from a detailed description of the technique of training in mindfulness developed by Sakyamuni Buddha, which was written down and called the *Satipatthana Sutta* (Pali). The term insight comes more easily, so it will be used.

Insight meditation is the basic first step in any Buddhist system of mind-training and is known in all schools of Buddhism. During the past sixty years it has become very popular among Westerners, and is now increasingly engaging the interest of Western psychologists because it is such a simple and safe path to transforming consciousness – enabling us to 'liberate' ourselves. Safe, that is, if it is correctly practised. Much of this book is an attempt to describe how to practise correctly (safely), this being necessary because, although the system is very simple, it takes one into areas of the mind which are often quite complex, confused and subversive. One needs to know how to deal with those conditions when meeting them.

Insight meditation is graduated and moves through distinct stages and phases, each one leading on and developing into the next. So we will begin at the beginning.

BARE ATTENTION AND MINDFULNESS

Mindfulness is based on *bare attention* and constitutes the most crucial aspect of meditation. 'Bare attention' is a good description, because when practising it, one's attention to the object of meditation is stripped bare. Initially we will not know what this means because we will not even be aware that our attention is not normally bare: we are so accustomed to the coverings that we do not know them for what they are. The greatest difficulty with bare attention is its simplicity: it is so simple that when we are practising it, we cannot actually believe that anything valid is happening: we are 'doing nothing' and in our busy lives doing nothing is usually regarded as an indulgent failure of energy and time conservation, or as a waste of time. But it is neither of these things. It is a highly alert and skilful state of mind because it requires one to remain psychologically present and 'with' whatever happens in and around one without adding to or subtracting from it in any way; like a movie camera – simply recording, with total accuracy and impartiality, what ever passes before the lens.

The first exercise entails 'watching' the breath. You can do it for yourself after reading the next few paragraphs.

Sit comfortably and ensure that you will not be disturbed for the next five tc ten minutes. Now, in a very relaxed way, focus your attention on the breath as it passes in and out of your nostrils. You obviously cannot see it, but you can feel it; there is a sensation of air moving through the nose and over the upper lip immediately below the nose. Do not alter or manipulate the breath in any way – you are simply using it as a focus for your attention because it is happening and will continue to happen while you are alive.

The quality of your attention is important. The word attention is deliberately used instead of concentration because it is not quite concentration. The latter implies something rigid and excluding. When one concentrates on something, one fixes one's mind rigidly and exclusively on that one thing, and disregards anything else that may be going on. After a while this action becomes tiring and impossible to hold without a great deal of training. Attention is lighter and more panoramic. When one attends to something, one arouses an interest in it, and a certain degree of fascination may be present. But there is no effort to hold the mind only on that and exclude all else. Like a cat watching a mouse-hole; there is keen attention there, but the cat also knows what else is going on around it. Someone walks by and there will be a flick of an ear or a glance, but the attention remains quite definitely on the mouse-hole.

So you rest your attention on the breath in a light and relaxed way, like a feather floating on a spring breeze. The consequence of this attention is that you become aware of something: aware of breath coming in, breath going out, breath coming in. This awareness arises naturally; you do not have to make any effort to gain it. This is your first discovery – attention gives rise to awareness: simple and obvious, but how few people know it! Continue attending to the breath and very soon you will make some more discoveries – there is a pause between the out-breath and the in-breath, and another pause between the in- and out-breath. Sometimes the in will be longer than the out and vice versa. Sometimes the breath will be strongest in the left nostril and sometimes in the right, and so on. You will become aware of many things you never knew before, not as a result of analysis or working out or complicated theorising, but simply as a consequence of attending to one thing – the breath.

But long before these discoveries are made, other things will have happened – mainly, your mind will have wandered. You will find that even before you have attended to the in and out of three or four breaths you will be thinking of something, or trying to work out the origin of a sound, or wondering whether what you are doing is a lot of nonsense, or something like that. When you become aware of this, there will usually be a reaction – 'Oh dear, I can't concentrate for more than a few seconds' or 'How on earth did I get here?!' or whatever – almost as though you have stepped out of the meditation and are now looking back so as to see where you went wrong. Mentally drop the reaction and return to the breath. Remember the movie camera – it simply records what is there without any form of reaction or comment. So if you are filming a flower and somehow miss your aim and end up filming a dung beetle, the camera will record the dung beetle without any trouble until you point it back at the flower.

This is what bare attention is about – attending simply to whatever occurs without any form of elaboration. So if your mind wanders from the breath, note the fact that that has happened, and return to the breath. If you are caught up with a sound, note it, and return to the breath. If your knee is hurting and you are wondering about that, note it and return to the breath. In every instance simply disengage without the need for drama or judgement, and return to the breath. So the attention is bare because one is keeping it always at a simple and primary level, simply recognising whatever is occurring without attempting to rationalise, judge, analyse or anything like that. Or, if you find you have got into any of these secondary activities, recognising that, disengage, and return to the breath. Bare attention can be regained at any point.

After a while you discover that bare attention is simply attending to all that occurs in relation to the senses – seeing, hearing, thinking and so on, acknowledging and letting go. If you persist in this practice you will find that it checks the flow of uncontrolled thought without your having to make an effort to do so, and without suppression. Of course, this effect will not be evident immediately, because we all have deep-rooted habits of allowing the mind to be rather wild and undisciplined, so you have to persist for a while before the mind begins to settle. Bare attention makes mindfulness possible.

Being mindful is being present in a knowing way with whatever is happening in and around oneself. It has a quality of taking note, but not in a heavy-handed or deliberate way. It is also a little like monitoring the continually passing panorama, but again with a light touch – not making a big issue out of it. A simile will help: think of the eye and the action of seeing. There is a physical eye which sees. The action of seeing is bare attention – images are reflected on the retina. Then the images are communicated to the brain which gives rise to the realisation or knowing that one is seeing. This is mindfulness. If it were not for this, one probably would not know whether or not one was seeing. Mindfulness is knowing from moment to moment what is going on. Again, at all levels, inner and outer.

Once you have understood bare attention and mindfulness, you can meditate. If what has been said seems too complicated or you feel unable to remember it, simply hang on to one phrase which will always bring you back into focus:

> *Meditation is knowing what is happening*
> *while it is happening,*
> *no matter what it is.*

This we can add:

> *Meditation is a state*
> *not an activity.*

So it is very simple: if you are sitting attending to the breath and you are present with the breath, you are meditating because you know what is happening while it is happening. If you gradually get lost in a daydream or doze off, you are no longer meditating because you do not know what is happening; if you are watching the breath and thoughts or emotions or sounds keep claiming your attention and drawing you away, you are still meditating provided you know while you are being drawn away that that is what is happening – because you still know what is happening while it is happening.

EXERCISE 1 : Bare attention

Practise bare attention for fifteen minutes as follows:

1. Find a quiet place and ensure that you will not be disturbed.
2. Sit on a comfortable seat with your back straight (a dining room chair is good).
3. Relax and focus your attention on the breath as described, 'flowing with the breath'.
4. Remain attentive to all that comes to notice – regardless of what it is. If you get lost in thought, as soon as you realise this has happened, disengage from the thought and return your attention to the breath.
5. Do this for five minutes and then have a short break. Then do two more five-minute spells and end your meditation session.
6. Throughout the day check whether or not you are being mindful – do you always know what you are doing while you are doing it? Meditation is not an isolated state. It is an integral part of our lives.

Continue this exercise for one week, gradually lengthening the period of your meditation until you are sitting for thirty minutes.

4

DISTRACTION

A scattered mind cannot accomplish even worldly activity;
so you need a calm mind, especially for dharma activity.
– Milarepa

When you begin to meditate, you will discover that the mind does not remain still; it constantly moves away from the object of meditation (the breath). This is the natural tendency of the untrained mind to scatter or be constantly wayward, like a wild horse that wants to roam the grassy plains. This condition is bound to be present and need not distress you. But with practice, and as you learn to understand the nature of distraction, the mind will begin to settle.

The essence of distraction is movement – movement away from the present instant. If you think about it, your living is never anything more than this instant: the only moment in the whole of eternity that you can actually experience is this moment – now; this place – here. If you were totally in the here and now, you would be totally alive, because you would be experiencing the totality of yourself, whatever that is. But we are almost never like that; we spread ourselves out psychologically in three main ways:

1. Following the past.
2. Thinking in the present, that is, becoming caught up with thinking activity.
3. Planning – getting drawn into the future.

Following the past

Much of our time is spent delving around in the past in a variety of ways: reliving happy, frightening, embarrassing or other significant experiences; re-running encounters with people and rationalising them, trying to work them out or just mulling them over; going on sentimental memory journeys and so on. Sometimes this activity of the mind can become so strong that it actually swamps us and blots out the present altogether – this is a form of insanity. But we all experience it to some degree at times. For example something might happen which has a great impact on one – perhaps one's partner leaves. This experience has an enormous emotional content so the memory of it, together with all the emotional implications, will tend to flood into the mind quite frequently and without invitation. Each time this happens the past will come alive. One finds oneself sucked back into the powerful memory which can be very painful. It's as though one is right back there at that moment of rejection and one is totally lost to the present. Some people spend an enormous amount of their time lost in this way. While one is in the past, one is not living; one is in a confused fog. Following the past leaves the mind weakened, confused, dull and scattered. The more this is done, the weaker the mind becomes.

When we meditate and thus begin to discover the degree to which we follow the past, we train the mind to let go and return to the object of meditation – the present moment. This letting go or dropping is an acquired technique and needs to be carefully understood. The tendency when one finds one's mind following the past, will be to get upset and condemn or judge the activity, viewing it as a failure. Having done this, one drags the mind back to the breath and attempts to expel the memory. The outcome is suffering and disturbance. This will cause feelings of guilt, anxiety and resentment to arise, thus further disrupting the meditation. So, approach the situation with care. Having become aware of the movement into the past, allow yourself to look at it in a very open accommodating way without being drawn into reactivity. That is the quality of letting go – simply to walk away psychologically from the object of distraction and quietly settle back to attending to the breath. The more this is done, the more settled the mind will become; clarity and tranquillity will begin to arise spontaneously.

Remember: what is past is gone; release it and relax fully into the present – the only time and place where one can be alive.

Thinking in the present

We are always thinking, and most of the time we are experiencing emotions. Generally when people think about meditation they imagine that the meditation technique will train them to throw a psychological switch which will cut off all this activity and leave the mind blank – hopefully, also calm, peaceful and blissful. This does not happen. Initially one will experience a continuation of the usual mental activity. What changes is the way one deals with it. Normally what occurs is this: one sits and focuses the attention on the breath. Very soon a thought arises. Before realising it, one becomes involved with the thought, gets caught up in it, and follows or develops it. For example, the thought of breakfast may arise in a very innocent way. Immediately one grasps hold of it and begins imagining fried eggs, toast, coffee and so on. Although one may not realise it, two distinct things have actually happened:

1. Thought about breakfast – which arises in an innocent, fresh and incipient form.
2. Elaboration or involvement. This is the actual thinking which constitutes distraction, and is a follow-on from the first.

The incipient thought arises and is gone in a moment. The elaboration can continue for minutes, hours, days or even years. It is this activity which we generally call 'thinking' and which holds us in bondage. It goes on and on and constitutes distraction when we are meditating because there is an element of conscious (or self-conscious) collaboration about it. There must be a certain amount of deliberate participation for it to continue. While it is happening we are 'lost' in thought, not fully 'present' in the here and now, and so not living to the full. Involvement with present thought leaves the mind weakened, confused, dull and scattered. The more it is done, the weaker the mind becomes. So we train ourselves to be free from this form of distraction in exactly the same way that we dealt with past thoughts – let go of or 'drop' the thought and return to the present. Once again, be sure to keep the mind open, loving and relaxed – no condemnation or denouncing of yourself. Simple disengagement is all that is necessary.

After a while a significant discovery will be made: one does not have to get caught up in thinking. It is possible to disengage from thought or feeling, let it drop, and experience the freedom of not being bound by the compulsion to go on thinking. This is a wonderful discovery! From time to time most people are caught up in whirling, recurrent thought patterns which repeat themselves endlessly. Psychologists call this obsession. When one is bound by obsessive thinking it can be exhausting, exasperating and eventually terrifying. Some people are totally incapacitated by it because they have no understanding of letting go, and actually believe that their thoughts have power over them. An astounding consequence of this training in meditation is the discovery that thoughts and emotions actually have no power at all. If one consistently practices the technique of letting go, one soon experiences this and subsequently enters into a state of freedom and peace.

Planning

This is inviting or getting drawn into the future. We spend an enormous amount of our energy in anxious planning or anticipation of things which have not yet happened and in fact, may never happen. This tendency will manifest strongly in meditation and constitutes the third form of distraction. It wastes energy and keeps the mind in a weakened and scattered state, just as the other two do. The same method is applied in dealing with this type of distraction – gentle disengagement and return to the object of meditation.

Disengaging from distraction

These, then, are the three categories of distraction. Because they are so deep-rooted in habit patterns, we are initially unaware of their existence. We vaguely sense a difficulty with concentration; our minds wander; we fantasise a lot. It is only when we start to cultivate mindfulness that we begin to recognise precisely what is happening and in particular, what effect it is having on every level of our lives. Many people complain of being 'untogether'. We all know how competent 'together' people appear to be, and how much happier they seem to be. When we meditate, the true significance of these observations becomes clear: a great deal of our suffering, and most of the difficulties in our lives are due to the fact that we are 'untogether', that is scattered; in a sense, not here. This means that most of the time we are simply unaware of our actions, blundering around in the dark hurting ourselves and others, spreading chaos and confusion wherever we go.

Furthermore, the scattered mind will experience a lot of turmoil, anxiety and guilt because it senses areas of unknown and unresolved complexes which it fears to approach. In the average person's mind this condition appears to be permanent. Generally we are so accustomed to this condition that we accept it as the norm. We do not know what to do about it, so we muddle on, using further distraction to rescue us from the effects of indulging in distraction. Hence our addiction to television, movies, loud noise, alcohol, drugs and the 'speedy' things that so characterise our culture. Why do we so desperately need all these stimuli? Because we cannot bear to be alone with ourselves. As soon as we are alone, the pain and turmoil begin to make themselves felt.

One begins to see now that meditation is a highly practical state. As one trains oneself in the art of letting go or releasing and combines it with the gentle attitude of allowing, a distinct change comes about in the mind. Through letting go, one systematically disengages from the habit of distraction – like curing oneself of an addiction. Gradually the mind begins to settle; it becomes calmer, more relaxed, open and joyous. As one proceeds, the tendency to become distracted subsides so that the number of thoughts and emotions streaming into the mind diminishes. At this stage one begins to experience real tranquillity, clarity and the beginning of insight.

Returning now to the essence of distraction – movement away from the present – one finds that a radical change manifests: the tendency to sidetrack the present ceases and one is able to be fully with oneself and with whatever is going on. This is radical because it is a life-changer. One shifts from fragmentation (the distracted mind) to integration (the fully-present, here-and-now mind). Because one is living completely in the present, the mind is no longer fragmented, that is drawn into areas extraneous to the present moment – reflecting on the past; elaborating the present; planning the future. The real wonder and significance of simply living-in-the-moment is experienced with the crystal-like clarity of a mind unclouded by distractions. This experience is not limited to periods of meditation, but permeates one's life.

This change will not come about suddenly, because one is dealing with life-long and powerful habits and patterns of distracted behaviour. But if one applies oneself seriously and consistently to the practise of mindfulness, then the effects will certainly manifest in meditation and in life generally.

With this change will come an understanding of the strong mind: a mind that is capable of remaining totally in the present moment without deflection or distraction.

EXERCISE 2: REMAINING IN THE PRESENT

Begin as for Exercise 1.

1. Spend the first ten minutes of the session relaxing and practising bare attention.
2. Have a short break, relax the body and look into space or out of the window for thirty seconds.
3. Return the attention to the breath as before, and practise bare attention.
4. Now begin to note specifically each time the mind wanders from the breath, how and where it has wandered:
   - i past thoughts
   - ii present thinking or fantasising
   - iii future planning
   - iv How did it begin moving away:
     - (a) in relation to some other stimulus for example a sound?
     - (b) as a result of a sensation?
     - (c) as a result of the spontaneous arising of a 'fresh' thought?
     - (d) other?

While noting in this way, see if you notice the difference between fresh thoughts and the thoughts that follow.

Continue this exercise for one week, making sure that you remain relaxed and easy in your mind. If you notice any signs of tension (tightness in the head or eyes, shoulders hunching up, jaws clenching and so on) stop meditating, gaze into space or out of the window for a while and leave off meditating for at least one hour.

EXERCISE 3: Meditation using sound

Traditionally breath is used as the focus for meditation, but this is not the only way and many people find other methods more beneficial.

If you live in a noisy place, or find that your mind is tense or tight or obsessive; or particularly if you find you are trying to control what is happening inwardly, or are too concerned with 'getting it right', you will discover that a subtle sense of struggle or striving will begin to dominate your meditation. This will cause the mind to become tense and rigid instead of pliable and open. The tense, rigid, striving mind is not meditating. It is the open, relaxed mind which experiences meditation.

If you are experiencing these difficulties, try using sound as the focus for your meditation.

Sit exactly as you did previously, but instead of focusing on the breath, allow your attention to relax into sound. This means, permit yourself to hear whatever sounds are coming to you, and allow your attention to remain with sound. You will soon discover the difference between hearing and listening. The latter is a tight, focused action which fixes on a chosen sound and attempts to remain with that to the exclusion of all others. This causes tension. Hearing is more panoramic and does not involve choice. Whatever sounds come to you are fine, and are choicelessly accepted as the focus for your mindfulness at any moment. The mind which is hearing will become relaxed and open, because there is no choice, preference or struggle – just an easy 'being present'.

Every time your mind wanders into distraction, see that this has occurred and return in a relaxed way to awareness of sound.

When meditating in this way, there is no need to do the noting exercise.

EXERCISE 4 : Short guided meditation

Start focusing your attention on the body. Simply allowing yourself to become fully aware of your body. Know what physical sensations are present. Know whether the body is at ease, or whether there is tension in it. Pain or discomfort. Just know that.

Feel the sense of pressure where your body is in contact with the ground or the chair. You don't have to analyse it, simply know it. Be aware of the sense of contact where one part of your body is in touch with the other. Just feel that. Allow yourself to experience the sense of these and the relaxation that arises when you realise that you are fully supported. The ground unconditionally holds and supports you. Therefore you can come to rest totally, without any effort. You don't need to strive.

Now let your mind fall softly into your body and let it come to rest. Think that your mind is held and supported by your body. Your mind has nowhere to go, nothing to do. It just comes to rest. You don't have to strive, you don't have to struggle to attain anything. Nothing to achieve. No fear of failure. You don't have to strive for any success. Let the mind rest in that way.

And now just let your attention open up to an awareness of sound. Let whatever sound arises command your attention without judgement. Without choice. Simply receive the sound and let that be your focus. As soon as the mind wanders, simply note that. And very gently, without force, return your attention to sound.

In the beginning, spend five or ten minutes in this way, simply relaxing in the presence of sound. Every time you realise your attention has wandered, return to awareness of sound, allowing whatever sound commands your attention to become the focus upon which your mind rests.

This is the basis for your training in meditation.

5

Regular Daily Practice

Whatever you can do, or dream you can, begin it.
Boldness has genius, power and magic in it.
– Goethe

If you want to introduce meditation into your life as a regular discipline, there are some basic principles which will be helpful.

Time

Reflect on your daily routine and work out when you can easily find time for meditation. Early morning is best, but if you cannot fit it in, then see when you can. Once you have fixed on a time, commit yourself to it, make it part of your daily schedule and keep to it. Meditation is cumulative so it is more important to meditate regularly for short periods than sporadically for long periods.

In the beginning, sit for fifteen or twenty minutes. Divide this period up into short sessions of five or ten minutes initially. As you become more accustomed to meditation, extend the time.

Never force or strain. If you become tired, have a break – relax, gaze out of the window for a few minutes.

Each week, extend the time of your meditation by five minutes until you get to one hour a day.

If you are able to manage two sessions a day, try to have one in the morning and the other in the evening. If you manage this, you could eventually be sitting for two hours daily.

Place

Select a place and go there every time you are going to meditate. Ideally it should be a room set aside for this purpose. If this is not possible, find a quiet place where you can sit without being disturbed. Keep it for this and no other purpose. Slowly a supportive atmosphere will build up.

Posture

In the long term posture becomes important, particularly if you are going to sit for long periods or go on retreats, so detailed instructions will be given. But in the beginning do not make too much of an issue of this. A beginner only need follow only two principles.

1. Sit comfortably
2. Keep the spine straight, preferably without leaning against anything. If you lean against a support you are likely to fall asleep. If you can sit cross-legged, that's good. If not, sit on a chair or stool with your feet resting on the ground.

Sitting

The ideal way of sitting will now be described – the lotus or vajra position. Very few people will be able to manage it straight away, so don't be disappointed if you cannot. Above all, do not attempt to force yourself into this posture. Be patient and kind to yourself. Tackle it little by little and allow your body to adjust and adapt slowly.

1. Feet – on opposite thighs. If in the beginning you cannot do this, you can begin by sitting 'tailor style'. After a while put the right foot up on the left thigh. As you loosen up, see if you can also get the left one up, on to the right thigh. Sit with right above left. In the beginning your knees will begin to hurt after a while. When the pain becomes too distracting, have a break and gently massage your knees.
2. Back – straight. Be careful not to have a concave bend in the lower back. Do not slump.

3. Shoulders – relaxed and pulled back a little, not hunched up around your ears.
4. Head – neck very slightly bent forward so that your eyes naturally look towards the ground ahead of you.
5. Hands – held in front of you, resting against the navel. Both palms up, left supporting right with the tips of the thumbs touching.
6. Tongue – relaxed, with the tip resting against the top teeth and the upper palate.
7. Eyes – ideally, kept open and defocused or looking in a relaxed way at a point twenty centimetres away from your nose. If you cannot manage this at the beginning then close them and slowly train yourself to keep them open.

In the beginning you will need a cushion about ten centimetres high.

CLOTHING

Wear loose clothing, especially on your legs. If you wear tight heavy trousers, they will bunch behind the knees and cut off blood circulation. This may happen even with loose clothing in the beginning. If it does, do not worry; your body will soon adjust.

Diet

Don't go on a trip about diet. Just eat a healthy balanced diet and avoid extremes.

Retreats and support groups

Retreats of one to ten days are very helpful and valuable. If you are planning on more than a day, look for a guide or experienced meditator to help you. Some people encounter psychological problems when they meditate a lot, so don't attempt too much on your own. If psychological material surfaces, this is usually a good sign because it means that deep-rooted purification is beginning. If you have really understood the principles of acceptance and self-compassion, you will be able to deal with anything. But most of us haven't, so help is valuable in the initial stages of practice.

It is also very helpful and valuable to meditate with a group. Group support helps us to keep going, and we are less likely to do silly things if we are meditating with others.

Finally

Meditation cuts through all the illusion, all the projection, all the confusion we have about others and mostly about ourselves. It is coming face to face with the mind and with what the mind is really about.

Understanding leads to penetrating insight into the illusion we have created for ourselves. This leads to liberation from suffering and a co-emergent manifestation of compassion and wisdom. But we do not see it as a goal. We let go of goals and we focus on the state of meditation.

Remember what Buddhism is all about – tolerance, loving-kindness, and compassion. Begin with yourself. Then begin training in compassion: begin every session by taking refuge; then reflect that through your efforts you want to help and benefit others. Meditate with this attitude; at the end of the meditation period, share what you have accomplished with all beings so that they too can be liberated from the wheel of suffering.

Acknowledgements

The most important thing about this book is the inspiration of my Gurus.

I wish to offer my deepest gratitude to Akong Tulku Rinpoche and Lama Yeshe Rinpoche without whom none of it would have been possible.

Karma Kagyu centres in Africa, Ireland and the United Kingdom

The Karma Kagyu is one of the four main traditions in Tibetan Buddhism. The Karmapa is the head of this lineage, brought to Tibet from India by Marpa in the 11th century.

Cape Town, South Africa
6 Morgenrood Road
7708 Kenilworth
Tel/Fax +27 21 7612978
capetown@kagyu.org.za
www.kagyu.org.za

Johannesburg, South Africa
43 Floss Street
2094 Kensington
Tel/Fax +27 11 6141948
johannesburg@kagyu.org.za
www.kagyu.org.za

Harare, Zimbabwe
Rokpa Harare & Chitungwiza
34 Quendon Road
Monavale
Tel +263 4 304202
Fax +263 4 308983
harare@kagyu.org.za
www.kagyu.org.za

Dublin, Republic of Ireland

KSD Buddhist Centre	Tel+353 1 453 7427
Kilmainham Well House	Fax +353 1 453 9312
56 Inchicore Road	info@buddhism.ie
Kilmainham, Dublin 8	www.buddhism.ie

London, England

London Samye Dzong	Tel +44 207 928 5447
Carlisle Lane (off Royal Street)	Fax +44 207 633 9339
Lambeth, London SE1	london@samye.org
	www.samye.org/london

Kagyu Samye Ling, Scotland

Samye Ling Tibetan Centre	Tel +44 13873 73232
Eskdalemuir	Fax +44 13873 73223
Dumfriesshire DG130QL	scotland@samyeling.org
	www.samye.org

More Buddhist centres in South Africa

The Buddhist Retreat Centre

PO Box 131	Tel 039 834 863
Ixopo 3276	brcixopo@sos.co.za
KwaZulu-Natal	www.brcixopo.co.za

The Dharma Centre

26 White Street	Tel/Fax 023 626 3515
Robertson 6705	dharmaken@worldonline.co.za
Western Cape	http://home.worldonline.co.za/~dharmaken

Emoyeni Retreat Centre

PO Box 190	Tel 014 574 3662
Mooinooi 0325	emoyeni@xsinet.co.za
North West Province	http://emoyeni-retreat.com

About the author

Rob Nairn is an internationally sought-after lecturer on Buddhism and meditation, and author of two more books: *Living Dreaming Dying – wisdom of Tibetan psychology* and *Diamond Mind – psychology of meditation*. His training in psychology and Buddhism – including a four-year isolation retreat at the Samye Ling Tibetan Centre in Scotland – enables him to translate ancient Eastern wisdom into concepts Westerners can understand and apply.

Rob has studied and practised Buddhist philosophy and psychology for over 40 years. Teachers include Khentin Tai Situpa, Thrangu Rinpoche, Akong Rinpoche and Lama Yeshe Losal Rinpoche. HH the 16th Karmapa instructed Rob to teach Insight Meditation. He thus resigned as professor of criminology at the University of Cape Town, South Africa, in 1979 to commit his life to the practice and teaching of the dharma – under the auspices of the Kagyu lineage and Rokpa Trust.

For information on Rob's courses and retreats internationally, see www.kagyu.org.za

About Rokpa Trust

Helping where help is needed

Rokpa Trust is an international family of charities founded by Dr Akong Tulku Rinpoche, which include humanitarian aid, healing arts and spirituality.

The spiritual activity of Rokpa and its many centres are maintained by Dr Akong Tulku Rinpoche and Lama Yeshe Losal Rinpoche, abbot and retreat master at Samye Ling.

Specialising in the living lineage of Kagyu teachings, perfectly preserved in Tibet for almost a millennium, the centres offer meditation and general counsel to people of all faiths, with the aim of promoting peace, spiritual well-being and compassion throughout the world including in southern Africa. For information on Rokpa Trust, see http:// www. rokpa.org